THE WALKING LEADER

THE WALKING LEADER

The 20 rules you can follow now to guide you down the path of leadership greatness in your organization

By David G. Guerra

David G. Guerra

The Walking Leader: The 20 rules you can follow now to guide you down the path of leadership greatness in your organization.

Subject headings:

Business – Leadership
Professional Development
Personal Growth

ISBN: 1492120065
ISBN-13: 978-1492120063

www.WalkingLeader.com/index.html

dave@daveguerra.com

Cover design by David G. Guerra.

First Printing: 2013
10 9 8 7 6 5 4 3 2 1

Table of Contents

Introduction

Many years ago, I heard the following story, which apparently, has been floating around since World War II:

While U.S. Army General George S. Patton was holding a press conference when one reporter made the mistake of asking the general how the war was going. Without missing a beat and in true Patton form, the general responded: "If you want to know how the war is going, go to where the bullets are flying."

This is such a great story and terrific advice to any manager and leader. No matter what industry you find yourself in, the only way for you to get a first-hand account of how things are going is to get out where things are happening. Walk among and talk with the men and women of the organization, especially those who are not in your department or area of responsibility.

Now, I ask every manager I run across: "How often do you go to where the bullets are flying?" Most of the time, I get the strangest looks because the majority of those managers have no clue as to what I am talking about. I explain the Patton story and point out exactly where the bullets are flying.

In a war, the bullets are flying at the frontlines. In a business – any business – the frontlines are where the employees and the customers meet every day. They meet at your organization's front counter, at the end of a telephone headset, at a visit to your office, on your website, Twitter interactions, Facebook posts. In fact, anywhere internal and external stakeholders interact is your frontline.

Remember: The only way to get a true 360° view of how the war is going in your organization is to get out from behind your desk or cubicle, grab your "battle gear" and venture out to the frontlines.

Originally, I was going to write this book for managers and leaders in government. However, as a recovering bureaucrat, I see the need exists in the private sector as well. As a result, it has taken me a little longer than expected to write this book. I have made adjustments here and there to ensure both the private and public sectors are covered. For the most part, this has been a labor of love in that it has taken quite a while to get here, but the journey has opened my eyes to see things and do things in an entirely different way.

As a member of the United States Army, I was trained to lead by example. As an Infantryman, I was trained to lead from the front. Now, as a Veteran, it is my turn to teach and train others to lead by example, to be leaders, and to be the ones out in front.

Knowing that we need to get out there, among the troops, is essential to becoming a great leader and not merely a mediocre manager. We have no choice; we need to get out among the employees and get to know them. Not only is it that simple but it is also mandatory.

Over the years while seeking more information on the topic of walking around and getting to know employees, I found that many leaders, authors and business communicators barely touch on the subject itself. All of them leave you, the reader or listener, with the feeling that you should already know how to do this. It is as if the moment you are given the title of "manager" and by some form of magic or osmosis you just know how to get out there and walk around. There is no magic. You have to learn how to do it and do it right. However, how you are expected to know how to get out there without being taught is beyond me.

Lacking the existence of any guide or guidance, I set out to create that guide, and wrote these twenty rules into a book so I can say to you, "Here you go. Go out there and do it, and if you need a guide, here it is!"

Over 25 years, I have seen massive changes take place in the public and private sectors either because of a change in the corporate culture or the economy dictating the direction a company takes, or military downsizing. During these changes one thing was constant, there were many great individuals who due to lack of direction or true leadership found themselves needing something or someone to focus on. That is where, as a leader, you have to step up. You have to take a stand and say to those on the frontlines that no matter what is happening around them, they still need a leader to show and tell them they are not only appreciated, but also that someone has their back and that someone is you. As leaders, it serves the organization the most when we can rally the troops enough that walking through fire becomes the norm and not the exception. This is why I wrote this book, because once the dust has settled, the true leaders will be the ones who will take their organizations to the next chapter of its existence.

Thus, I present to you "The Walking Leader", a collection of twenty rules you can follow to help you lead from the front and make you a stronger, well-rounded asset to your organization, group, department or team.

"The Walking Leader" is written to be used and immediately implemented by anyone – whether you are in a management position or not. "The Walking Leader" is for you, only if you want to better understand what the organization is doing and how acquiring this knowledge can make you a stronger leader. Don't those that follow you deserve a stronger leader?

Remember, leaders can come from any location or position within the company. That means you do not need anyone's permission to be that leader. So, why not become your organization's next leader – a strong, empowered and informed leader.

IMPORTANT: I recommend you read the entire book before you start putting these twenty rules into action. By reading the entire book, you get a better feel, understanding of what the Walking Leader is all about, and how you can customize the twenty rules to your unique situation.

Who Is A Walking Leader?

In most simple terms, the Walking Leader is you.

You are the Walking Leader. I never intended for the Walking Leader to be a program or system. Quite the contrary, it has to be a way of life. It has to be something that you incorporate into your daily existence. You will take these twenty rules and roll them into what you are doing now.

Unlike programs and systems that call on you to replace what you are doing with what they want you to do. You are augmenting what you are already doing. You are making what you do better. There will be a few changes but these changes are subtle and over time you will not notice the changes happening.

The Walking Leader is someone who knows that to be an effective and caring leader is to get to know the people that make the organization what it is. The Walking Leader is also someone who knows that they do not know everything and is not afraid to ask questions to get the answers. The right answers. The right answers from the right people.

Do not be afraid to get out from behind your desk. Do not worry about the *cool kids*; remember they are all just going with the grain. Go against that grain and let the *cool kids* worry about themselves. I know what you are thinking, "but the *cool kids* will make it difficult and they will talk." Let them!

People will always talk. That you cannot change so let them. What you can change is how they talk about you. You and your actions mixed with your authenticity can change the bad to good and vice versa. A word (or two) of warning, it is easier to change from good to bad than it is to go from bad to good. Be careful how you proceed and what you do.

I am not saying that you should abandon everything for fear of what someone might say. Quite the contrary, I am advocating that you get out there and prove it to yourself that you can do it whether people talk good, bad, both or neither about you. You get out there and do it for yourself and nobody else. You do it for YOU!

However, do listen to what your boss has to say. Your boss, if she is a Great Boss or an Excellent Leader will work with you to ensure that you stay focused and do not stray too far from your primary tasks. Remember, any Leader worthy of the title of Leader will do everything she or he can to ensure that followers succeed in the organization and in their personal life.

Thus, in a nutshell I offer this:

- Stay Focused.

- Do your work first.

- Do not be afraid of what others think or say.

- Cast your personal fears and phobias aside.

- Get out there!

There is nothing more I can say or write to motivate you to get out there and start walking on your organization's front lines. You are the Walking Leader! Now get out there and act like it.

Rule #1
Do It To Everyone

When I was starting to be a Walking Leader, I just could not see all the organization's employees. They would be working the overnight shift from 10:00pm to 6:00am and I was on the regular 8:00am to 5:00pm shift. The state agency I worked for had 24/7 operations, which meant there were four work shifts. I regularly saw the 6:00am to 2:00pm and the 2:00pm to 10:00pm shifts, along with the 8-5 crowd. To be true to what my intention was, to reach everyone within the organization, I adjusted my work schedule to ensure that I was able to see everyone in the organization, especially the overnight shift. As a department head, I had the flexibility to change my work schedule to ensure that I was able to spend time with as many of employees as possible. Getting out there and having access to all the work shifts was one of the best things I could do as a supervisor, as a manager, as a leader.

The first rule will always be the "Golden Rule" of The Walking Leader: **DO IT TO EVERYONE**. This is not negotiable otherwise do not do it at all. You are a leader of many, not a leader of one select group of people – no matter whether you supervise the people you walk around and see or not. If you identify yourself only as someone in charge of a select group of people, well, you are just a "manager" or "supervisor," not a leader. I truly believe that anyone can manage people, but not just anyone can lead. As for being a supervisor, you are a manager and please re-read the previous sentence.

By walking around the entire organization ensures that you, as a leader, do not appear to be playing favorites by spending time only with your department or group. Of course, those in your department or group will always be your primary concern and should get priority treatment, but when you step outside your area of responsibility, things tend to change focus and priority. Therefore, use caution when you are mobile. If you have been in the business world for more than five minutes then you have all too often seen nothing can ruin a leader's credibility and reputation faster than being perceived as someone who is always playing favorites. On the other hand, your subordinates will not feel they are being picked on, because they will see that you are doing it to everyone and not only in your department or section's area of operation.

When you venture outside your department, be careful that outsiders see you as not just trying to "work the room," but as being genuine in your intentions. Failing to do this will certainly lead to more problems than to resolutions.

Initially, some people will be curious as to why you seem to be everywhere. This is natural; there is nothing wrong with getting what appears to be the *third degree*" from your subordinates, peers, superiors and other interested parties. However, staying the course and behaving the same way with everyone might limit you to get just the first and second degrees. However, if you continue to be pressed about what you are doing, your response should be that you are simply walking around and getting to know co-workers and the operations of the company. You will not be lying.

Eventually, as this habit of walking around develops, the curiosity and trepidation around your presence will be replaced by the expectation of seeing you walking around. At this point, what you are doing has been accepted and the expectation of you walking around the organization has now become part of your organization's culture. If you are one of the first individuals in your organization to walk around and you have reached the level where people expect to see you doing it, then it is time to start recruiting others to do their own walking around – to become the organization's next Walking Leader.

It might be easier than you think to get others involved in venturing out to the frontlines to see how the war is going. They will know how the war is going first-hand because they will be out there where the bullets are flying. They will see and feel the heat, sweat and emotions that are part of the day-to-day operations of the organization on all fronts. They will see what is real and be able to compare that to the data that is more than likely presented in cold, sanitized emails and projected on screens during those PowerPoint-fueled monthly status meetings.

Rule #2
Do It All The Time

At first, I found it easy to get out there every day. I was excited to walk the facility grounds, enter all 16 buildings, and visit the four remote sites. Then, as time passed, I found it difficult to get out there every day. That is when I again rearranged my schedule to accommodate my walks. Unfortunately, something had to give and that was my visits to the remote sites. My ability to travel was now limited to the three closest sites, which I visited once a week, and the farthest site, which I got to once or twice a month. As the most remote site was more than 150 miles away, it required an overnight trip, so it became a two-day visit. Thus, I really tried to spend an almost equal amount of time at all the field sites. It was difficult at first to ensure that everyone got the same level of support and attention. However, over time, it became easier to work into the schedule and whether they knew it or not, the remote sites ended up getting support priority over the local site.

The second rule: *DO IT ALL THE TIME* goes hand in hand with Rule #1. You could say that together they share the title of the "Golden Rule" of the Walking Leader. This rule, much like all the others, is self-defined in that you set the level and standard of when and how you do it.

To maintain your credibility and to develop a genuine habit, DO IT ALL THE TIME must be followed without fail. Doing it all the time ensures you can be counted on to be out there on the frontlines. Whether it is the same time every day or spread out throughout the day, the rule is just that simple: Be out there all the time. This does not mean you should be out walking for your entire eight-hour or 12-hour shift. It means you have to incorporate it as part of every workday. It also means that your mission and your area of responsibility must take priority over anything that you do as a Walking Leader.

While you are out there doing it, I advise to be random as there is no need to go in one direction all the time. Shake it up, mix it up and stir it up. It does not matter where you begin, or which way you go. What does matter is that you just get out there.

Early in my Walking Leader process, I forced Walking Leader time into my calendar. This was to ensure I had the time scheduled, to avoid over-scheduling, and to create a pop-up reminder to get me out to do it. To be clear: My role in the organization was that of a manager of a small department. However, I viewed as a leader within the organization nonetheless. Therefore, it was in my best interest to get out there and be out there constantly and consistently.

In my case, I was responsible for a small department of three that ensured the uptime of the most critical components of the organization: Information Technology. This, by default, made my staff and me some of the most important people in the entire organization. Therefore, the need to get out there was driven by the need to ensure the equipment was functional and used in the way it was meant to be used. Of course, along the way I met and talked to people (the employees). This in itself is priceless, especially when a new manager needs to ensure that when it comes time to rally the troops, they will do so without hesitation. The troops will find it easier to rally around someone they know, trust and respect as opposed to someone who demands respect just because the individual has a title.

Being a Walking Leader does not mean you are allowed to shirk your primary responsibilities. Being a Walking Leader means you are augmenting and enhancing your duties and responsibilities. Performing your primarily duties and responsibilities, what you were hired to do, must never suffer because you would rather be out walking around. Over time, as you get out there, you will see that it makes your primary responsibilities a little easier to handle as you can catch things before they get out of hand (more on this later) and even improve on things that are already happening.

Rule #3
Go By Yourself

As a department head, sometimes an employee or two would want to tag along during my walks. They were curious about what I was discovering, especially when I walked through their areas of responsibility. While under normal circumstances, I would welcome company on the walk this was not a normal circumstance, it was a special situation. Tactfully, I spoke to the members of my department and explained what I was doing and why I was doing it. They understood and did in fact let me walk alone. However, I could feel them keeping an eye on me whenever I ran into them during the walk. To put them at ease I would walk up to them and talk to them. It was difficult for them to not follow me but they respected what I was doing and understood that to really get this to work I had to be free to roam.

Go by yourself. You are an adult. You have been able to cross the street by yourself for some time now. You should really have no problem going by yourself. If you find that you have issues going anywhere by yourself then you might not be where you really truly belong. Being a Walking Leader is something that can only be done by yourself. Do not be tempted to ask for a buddy to tag along. Remember your authenticity is at stake.

What do you think is more dangerous: crossing a street or walking around your workplace? If your place of work is an insurgent-filled street and you carry an M60 machinegun, then taking that walk would be best with an 11-man infantry squad that has your back. In a typical workplace, however, you can bet that crossing a street is more dangerous. So, don't sweat walking alone!

Of course, you will be tempted to go with a friend or others of the management team. You can do this, but make certain the moment you leave your office everyone walks in different directions.

Walking around the organization by yourself has inherent benefits, such as:

- you are by yourself
- you are 100% there (present in the moment)

- you are approachable

Being approachable means no one has to wonder if you are busy or do not want to be disturbed. You are there to be approached! It is human nature to hold back when others are present. If the intent of having a conversation is to ensure a successful exchange of information, ideas and concepts, then it can be done without a third, fourth or fifth person with you watering down the conversation.

Being 100% present in the moment means there are no distractions. So do limit what you carry. If you are truly 100% in the moment as a Walking Leader, you cannot be fidgeting with your tablet, iPad, iPhone, smartphone, Blackberry, or cell phone. Seriously, how can anyone be 100% in the moment if they are chatting on the phone or waiting for Facebook to reload on the iPad? Not so long ago, I came across some information that suggested people who say they are good at multi-tasking are giving no more than 80% of their attention to the tasks they are attempting to multi-task.

How does 80% translate into being 100% present? It does not! Either you are 100% here in the moment, or you are not. It is like being pregnant. Either you are pregnant or you are not; there is no middle ground whatsoever. Yes, I understand there are very big differences between being pregnant and being a manager or being a leader. I also understand that all require 100% commitment. Do you see where I am going with this? The ability to be present and in the moment with those you encounter while walking around the organization will increase your level of authenticity and most certainly deepen your understanding of those with whom you interact. Both of which are a good thing.

Being present, without any distractions, will always be a matter of committing to something that will make your life as a leader better. Otherwise why bother? Of course, if people are looking for you they will have to do it the old-fashioned way and walk around until they find you. Trust me on this one; it is better if you come to them and not the other way around.

Do not be tempted to travel in a pack. Be daring, be bold and go out there by yourself. Constantly and consistently being by yourself during your walks helps to project the seriousness and the commitment of what you are trying to accomplish as a Walking Leader. Therefore, in order to be continually improving yourself and making yourself a stronger leader within the organization you must do everything you can to ensure you are out there by yourself.

TIP: In order to be effective as a Walking Leader you will need to carry a few things with you, ALWAYS. First, carry a note pad; keep it small enough to fit in your pocket. I highly recommend the Field Notes pocket notebooks, as they are the most accessible and portable that I have ever seen and used. Next, you will need two ink pens. Red, blue, black or green. It does not matter, as long as you have two different ink colors with you at all times. Why two colors? One color is for regular note taking and the other is for critical, important and urgent notes and comments. The last thing to carry is a watch or a timepiece. Not only will you need to keep track of your time but when taking notes, time stamp everything your write. It will help you when it comes time to putting into action what you have written.

Rule #4
Do Not Circumvent Any Manager, Ever!

Imagine for a minute you are in your department talking to your employees when a manager from a different department comes in and starts to tear into one of your staff members. You certainly would not like that. I know I did not. In fact, I was fit to be tied. How dare this individual walk into my department and start going off on a member of my staff? I do not recall what the issue was but I do remember I had to raise my voice at that manager just to get his attention. I quickly made it clear that my staff is not his staff, and if there was any problem, he should bring it me or my immediate supervisor, who just happened to be two levels up the organizational chart from this manager. There is protocol no matter what or where you are, you cannot forget that. However, this manager decided he was not going to be bothered with protocol. Ultimately, he had to answer for his actions while standing in front of the facility director and was reminded that there are certain expectations that must be met by all managers.

Nothing makes a manager look like someone who is in it solely for himself or herself than one who circumvents another manager, especially if the other manager is from a different department. If you believe being a Walking Leader is your opportunity to "out-manage" a manager from a different department or a front-line supervisor, then please consider yourself wrong. Nothing will cause you to lose face faster than going out there and trying to manage everything that is happening, especially in departments or sections that are not in your primary area of responsibility. For Pete's sake do not ever do that. Of course, there are a few exceptions; however, these should be rare and far between – like saving a life.

Before you go out and about, know you are there to observe and interact with the people you meet, and not to disrupt the workflow. Once you are out there you may be tempted to start running the show. However, do not forget you are not to stay out on your walks for hours on end; you are to be on the move, always. Be like water in a babbling brook and not water in a still pond. Water that is running is good water while water in a still pond is not good, maybe even rancid. This means that any "managing" that takes place – while it may be for a few seconds – will have long-lasting repercussions. Those managers' toes that you are stepping on will resent you, they will start to lose faith in your leadership ability, and they will start to question your decisions and your "true" motives and intentions for walking around the organization, most of all.

All managers in your organization are there for a reason. They became managers because someone had the faith they could do something right and beneficial for the organization. If those managers do not have what it takes to be managers then you, as a manager, would still be out on the frontlines. See, the people that hired them to be managers also hired you. So cut them some slack and let them do what they were hired to do. In the meantime, remember not to cross over to the dark side and be tempted to act on putting in your two-cents. Stay grounded and secure in the knowledge that those front-line supervisors are doing the job they were hired to do and you are doing what you were hired to do.

Yes, there are exceptions on when to interfere, as I mentioned. In an emergency, it is understood that you will intervene and assist. There are other times when interventions are necessary. A lot will depend on your gut instincts. As always, if something does not feel right, get all the facts (or as many as immediately possible), make a decision, and then ACT. While I might not be telling you anything new, I am reinforcing the fact that as a leader within your organization, you have the right to ensure that things are going the way they should. After all, isn't that why you are out there in the first place?

Rule #5
Ask Questions

During my seventeen years working for the State of Texas, I had the opportunity to get to know many people. I knew them and they knew me. At one point, it was more as if they knew of me and I knew of them. However, there were many people at our state headquarters who somehow learned who I was through reputation (a good one, I hope), when I would go to Austin and walk down the halls they would say "Hello, David" and I would say "Hello" back to them. At first, I thought it was cool that people knew of me, but after several visits, it started to get a little creepy. Here were people that knew of me but I had never seen or talked to before, until one day, I decided it was time to ask: "Excuse me, but how do you know me?" The response floored me: "Oh, everyone in the IT department speaks so highly of you, you are like a legend. You know the guy that everyone talks about but never sees." Asking just that one question let me know that I must be doing something right.

Asking Questions is not only a great way to know what is happening but is also another great rule that you should adhere to always. This is where your notepad and pen come in handy. At a minimum, when you are out there be certain that you are asking these important questions:

- How are you?

- How's the family?

- How's work?

- Is there anything you feel is important that I should know?

If you do not know how long someone has been with the organization, ASK! Really, it is OK to ask. However, please write their answer down so next time you will not look like an insensitive, uncaring pinhead when you ask the same person the same question. A little harsh, but it has to be stated and re-stated: write it down! I once had a direct supervisor ask me four times in one year how long I had been with the organization. By that last time, I told him I started two months ago. He looked at me, raised his eyebrow, and never asked me that question again. If I came across as a smart aleck then so be it, but I got my point across.

If you really want to get to know the employees then here is something you can ask: "Since you have been here <<*enter duration here*>>, is there anything you see that needs changing?" If it seems there are more answers than expected, then ask for one item on the list, the one thing that is most important to that individual. Write the answer down.

For the most part, everyone has at least one pet peeve or something they do not like about the way things are done within the company, department or unit. I know I do and I know you do. However, hearing it from the front-line staff carries more weight than hearing it from a local administrator.

Why?

The front-line staff has to do the job whether it is someone's pet peeve or not. They are the ones stuck doing the dirty job whether they like it or not. Therefore, they are the ones that know when things work, when they do not and when those things need changing.

Take out your *Field Notes* notebook and jot down their answer and comments. Do not promise you can change anything but say only that you will see what you can do about it. You can and must promise that you will move it up your chain of command. Do not fail them; above all else keep this promise. Do not fail them and most of all do not fail yourself.

When you start collecting the "pet peeve" or complaint information from the staff there are a few things you must do to ensure that you are not on a *snipe* hunt. You will have to use your powers of deduction along with your management and leadership skills to take the information they gave you and determine whether it is valid or not. Valid in the sense that you must make certain the staff member is not just complaining for the sake of complaining.

A word of caution: Just like a rumor, every complaint has some form of truth to it, so each complaint must be explored without fail. This lends itself to building interest and authenticity among your peers, superiors and especially those you supervise. *Never neglect entering those collected concerns into the proper channels for processing, and hopefully to ensure that some kind of appropriate action is taken.*

I do not have to tell you how much damage your credibility will take if you fail to report the concern or the truth found within the complaint. Do not find yourself short-changing those who what put their trust in you. Remember, once damaged you may never get the credibility you once had the honor of possessing.

Once you have this under complete control then you are ready to go ask questions. Do not forget to write down the answers to the questions you had previously asked.

As a by-product of your walks, you can address issues that have the potential to save your organization time, money, litigation and quite possibly a life. Also, please realize that you are not Don Quixote and you cannot solve all the problems in one day or week.

About Don Quixote, do not forget he went charging at "dragons" that were actually windmills. Know exactly what the problem is and what it is not! You still have your job to do, so realize that your crusade must remain focused and centered, and not directly affecting the performance of your primary job function and duties. You will be tempted to step right in and fight a fight that is not yours to fight. Be careful. Remember, you are working hard to ensure others take you seriously in what you are doing and what you want to accomplish during your walks. Be informed, Ask Questions, and Pick your battles wisely.

Rule #6
Look...Listen...Learn

Throughout my Basic and Advanced Training as a U.S. Army Infantryman, all the Drill Sergeants and Instructors worked hard to make certain we fully understood three things to succeed as Infantrymen: To Look, To Listen and To Learn. This came in handy numerous times throughout my military career and continues to serve me in civilian life. My first duty assignment was to the U.S. Army Berlin Brigade in what was then West Berlin, Germany, and it would turn out to be the best adventure of my entire adult life. I was fresh out of Basic and Advanced Infantry Training (AIT), so I knew what my job entailed. What I did not know was how to do it in the "Berlin Brigade" way. The ONLY way I was going to find out how to do this was to Look and Listen and Learn. Luckily, when I first arrived, a couple of great Commissioned and Non-Commissioned Officers helped guide me. As well, several of my peers who were all still green but who had a few weeks ahead of me and that made all the difference. It took me about a month after my arrival to be fully up to speed with everyone else. Of course, I made mistakes but I made them once (rarely twice) and then learned from those mistakes.

Look…Listen…Learn. Remember why you are out there walking around your organization. You are out walking around not just to be seen but also to get to know how the *"war is going"* to see your organization's ambassadors doing their thing and, of course, to learn from them. Go out there with open eyes, open ears, an open mind, and in almost all cases a CLOSED mouth. Leave your "manager glasses" in the office and put on your "Leader glasses." This may sound easy, but it is quite the opposite, especially around week three or four of constantly walking around.

Why week three or week four? This is when the novelty of the new shiny object usually starts to wear off. There can be no slacking off when it comes to being a Walking Leader. Never.

Once the novelty of walking around your organization starts to dissipate, it will be easy to slip back to manager mode, and the next thing you know, you are calling this "adventure" a complete failure. However, now is the time to kick things into overdrive. Dig deep inside yourself and recognize there is no other way to accomplish what must be accomplished, and that is to get a realistic picture of the organization: A snapshot of how the company is doing and what it can do to get better. There is no other way to get the true sense of how the employees – at all levels – really feel about their jobs, their peers, their supervisors, the company's leadership, the client or customer, and especially how they feel about the entire process. There is no other truly effective way than to get out there and look, listen and learn.

Look

Look at what is happening all around. A complete 360! Be extra vigilant when it comes to looking at the details. In the details, you will find areas of concern that must be addressed before they grow into big problems. These areas of concern can vary in location and size. They can come in the form of someone cutting a corner here or there, or a bad habit starting to develop in the customer service side of the operation. Remember, all clients are different; no two are the same. However, basic customer service skills and methods have a common beginning. The sooner you can spot these areas of concern, the sooner you can address them.

Listen

Listen to the people. Listen to the equipment. Listen to the birds. Are they chirping? Remember Rule #5: Ask Questions? Well, please take the time and listen to the answers. Listen carefully and, if you have to, please repeat back what you were just told. It is OK. After all, you are trying to make certain you completely understand what is being said. This ensures that you are listening and not just hearing people speak (*cue the adults speaking in those Charlie Brown holiday specials.*) Listening and understanding reinforces to the employee that you have connected with them 100%. Take notes and, when possible, write down exactly what the employee says. This will help get the ball rolling much faster than if you are trying to recall what the sixth person you talked to today said.

Learn

As for learning, well, this is something that comes with time. By this, I mean that as you start to look and listen you will gain more knowledge and experience on how things are done. You will learn how they are being done the right way and you will most certainly identify the wrong way of doing things. You will also then be better prepared to call upon that knowledge and wisdom to make informed decisions that are valid and sound all the time, not just when you are walking around. You will start to learn about the skills, abilities, and the driving force that each employee brings to the organization. Who knows? You might just find a diamond in the rough!

Rule #7
Share Well With Others

Communicating information with others is critical in any high-intensity situation. When situations are unfolding, the ability to share information is that much more essential. In the summer of 2008, Hurricane Dolly was bearing down on South Texas. As the lead Regional IT person for the agency where I worked, it fell on my staff and me to ensure that ALL networking equipment was taken offline, secured and ready to return to service after the storm had passed. This was definitely going to be a daunting task, as we not only had to secure the 16 buildings at the primary facility but also the four remote sites, while also ensuring that my staff was back home in time to take care of their personal property and be with their families during the storm. Well, somehow, some way, before Hurricane Dolly arrived, everything we were able to plan and prepare for worked the way it was supposed to work out. Throughout the entire process, we were communicating with ALL the sites, our central office in Austin, and with the local staff, to ensure that everyone knew when data communication would be terminated at each *site so that it could afford the longest possible uptime as well as provide safe travels to and from home for my staff. Luckily, everything went off without a hitch. Hurricane Dolly came and went with minimal damage to any of the agency's structures. Aside from a few flooded roads, all the equipment was re-connected as quickly as possible.*

Always be certain to share everything you can with others. Share what you can and when you can. However, you should know and let everyone else know that you are not there to get anyone in trouble and you will only reveal what you can reveal. While you are there to see others, to be seen, and to be available, at some point you are going to have to talk to others about what you have seen, heard and learned. This can get tricky, especially at first, but do not give up or feel that you have to hold back. Once you are well entrenched in your walking around, talking to others about what you have encountered will become easy.

Once people know and understand, your intentions are nothing more than to benefit the organization, things will run more smoothly. Sadly, getting to that point can be a long and bumpy road, please be patient, and whatever you do, do not give up. Never give up!

Although it will take a while to get the dialogue between you and those around you to flow smoothly, it should not hinder you from sharing the information you have acquired. If you ask yourself, with whom should you share this information? The answers is quite simple: EVERYONE.

At a minimum, you should share with your supervisor and the heads of the departments you are reporting on. Of course, some information cannot be shared with everyone. This type of information ranges from violations of company policies and procedures to criminal activities. Depending on the situation and the severity, the dispersion of the information must be unconditionally compartmentalized. Do the best you can to ensure that sensitive information is handled no further down (or across) the chain of command than it needs to be. I cannot stress enough that in highly sensitive situations information must be shared only with those that have a need to know.

What are you sharing?

You share EVERYTHING: the good, the bad and, of course, the ugly – no matter how ugly it turns out to be. This means you cannot go around pulling any punches. It also means that you not only have to be genuine to the ones who see you walking around, but you have to be authentic to the people you are sharing the information with.

Above all, you have to remain true to the people you are talking about. At some point, some of them will feel you are the only conduit to the top, to management, and you had better be delivering the goods consistently and accurately EVERY time!

The rule of SHARE WELL WITH OTHERS is also a shining example of why it is so very important to take accurate notes. When you are passing along the information you have picked up during your walks, having specifics and sometimes even exact quotes from those you talked to is priceless. Your intent is not to become a snitch but to become someone who will not pull punches nor distort the facts when it comes to sharing or presenting that information. Failing at this, as previously mentioned, will certainly lead to credibility and authenticity issues, which once damaged are very difficult to restore.

Rule #8
Try Out Their Work

The military has a funny way of training people. They cross-train everyone on just about any and every job the military offers. One day, I would find myself qualifying on my M16 rifle at the firing range, and the next I would receive training on how to remove obstacles from roads or applying a field dressing to a sucking chest wound. Removing obstacles from roads is the primary responsibility of combat engineers, not infantrymen. The sucking chest wound is something a medic should be called upon when the situation presents itself. However, in a critical situation a combat engineer or a medic might not be available. Thus, it serves my team, my unit, and me to know what to do or at least have some of the fundamentals down. I now employ that same cross training in my professional life. At first, I would hear the old "that's not my job," but persistence pays off. Now all of my organization's employees know what it takes to fill in gaps when someone is out sick or takes a vacation.

Try out their work. Do not just stand around and look at what people are doing. Roll up your sleeves, get in the trenches and find out first-hand what they are doing. Get a first-person point of view of their unique perspective of how the war is going. Fill a few sandbags, dig that foxhole and fire a few rounds downrange. What I am saying is see what they see, feel what they feel, touch what they touch, and do what they do (if you can).

Do not forget: When safety regulations call for ONLY certified individuals to do the job, then you must not interfere with the performance of those specific duties. Make sure you do not do anything to compromise the execution of those duties. Ask questions and observe but do not get in the way and most of all, do not touch anything.

Whenever you can please step up, step in and do their job. Try out their work with enthusiasm and be genuinely interested. Otherwise, why bother? While you might not become proficient enough to take over their job within the organization, you will gain the basic skills and knowledge to know how things work and how they should be done. This will become extremely handy when, in the future, someone is trying to pull the wool over your eyes, because you will have the upper hand. Seriously, possessing the ability to know what's what out on the frontlines will generate greater respect for you and for what you are doing as part of your walks.

While not all jobs are created equal, the ability for one individual to do as many of them as possible is priceless to the organization. In the public or private sectors, being a cross-trained member of the organization will help almost anyone advance within the organization. Additionally, consider it another feather in your cap when it comes time to venture out to find employment with a different organization. Having a broad skill set makes a manager – any manager – a highly sought-after individual, as well as a jewel worthy of retention and doing what it takes to keep that individual on the payroll is priceless. This is, of course, a by-product of trying and learning how others do their jobs.

As mentioned, some jobs can be done only by certified individuals. Does this mean you cannot try doing their job? It means you can shadow them unless the issue of confidentiality comes into play and you do not have a need-to-know or the security clearance, then the answer is a resounding "No!" Otherwise, get out there, now.

Rule #9
Bring good news

The old adage of no one wants to be the bearer of bad news is true, for the most part. Sure, there are sadists who like that kind of stuff. However, there is nothing wrong with bringing good news when you can. In 2010, in Deep South Texas we were under a hurricane warning, which meant we were in the projected path of then Hurricane Alex. One thing that kept everyone on edge was that at the time of the warning, Alex had been upgraded from a Tropical Storm to a Category 1 hurricane and the final point of landfall had yet to be fully determined. Once the warning was issued, my state agency's support staff kicked into overdrive to prepare to shut down all operations at all facilities that were to be affected by the landfall of a hurricane. I had made my initial walk through all the buildings and locally based remote sites. One could feel the apprehension and uncertainty of the impending storm, what to do, and when to do it. I knew my presence was not comforting because it meant, to them, that we were going to shut down operations. At some point during the walks, I received a call telling me that from the look of things there was no need to shut down operations as all the structures were rated to withstand winds in excess of 100 mph. Category 1 hurricanes have a top wind speed of 95 mph. The Weather Service predicted the storm would not intensify to Category 2 or higher. As I was out and about, I took the opportunity to let people know there was going to be no shutdown of operations. The look of relief that came over people was priceless. The employees felt so relieved that they did not have to worry about closing down the agency's operations while concerned about securing their families, homes and property. These times of bringing good news are few and far between, but when you have the opportunity, take it. By the way, Hurricane Alex turned west, made landfall on the east coast of Mexico, and briefly made it to Category 2. On the Texas side of the storm, winds never exceeded 45 mph at any of our facilities.

Bringing Good News to those you see in your walks is always a good thing and a great morale booster. The ability to boost morale is an essential characteristic that all leaders must not only possess but fully control and master. Why not boost morale when you take your walks? Bringing good news can be a little tricky because what is good news to some might not be good news to others.

However, with a little tact and good implementation of your decision-making skills you will be able to pick and choose when and what information you will share. As a leader, this skill is one you should be working on constantly to master but know that mastery will never be achieved.

If the latest news is old news, that's OK. Bring what you have and deliver it in a way that calls on staff members to reflect on the news – such as asking them what they think. Get their views and insights. Then again, it is also acceptable to bring no news. However, remember: Never ever bring bad news, especially to another department.

About the bad news.

No one likes or wants to be the bearer of bad news so do not be "that" person. Of course, as a leader you will have plenty of opportunities to deliver bad news. When you do so you should ONLY deliver it to those, you directly supervise just as other supervisors do to those they supervise. After the bad news – no matter what it is – has had a chance to be disseminated across the organization you must be prepared to deal with the fallout

as you walk the frontlines. The fallout will usually be in the form of individuals or groups wanting to talk to you about what is happening or has happened. Count on it to happen as asking for more information is human nature. Be prepared to deal with the issues or questions that individuals from other departments will ask. If the content they wish to discuss is too deep or you are just not comfortable talking to them about it, then you must absolutely, positively direct them to their direct supervisor.

What if the bad news does not apply to the organization as a whole? What then? Consider this: What if the bad news was mandatory unpaid furloughs for one-quarter of the workforce and permanent layoffs for another quarter of the workforce? Now, your department got off easy and only has to deal with one individual who gets the unpaid furlough. The rest of the departments in the organization have the layoffs and furloughs distributed evenly. Obviously, you can listen to those who talk to you on your walks but you are not the one who will be delivering the bad news, nor is there anything directly you can do to effect a change in the situation. That is for their supervisors or managers to handle directly.

However, as is the case in almost all organizations, bad news has a tendency to leak before it can be disseminated effectively. These leaks create problems such as the propagation of rumors, which once let loose, are extremely difficult to reign in. Remember, as you go forth among the masses, you will be asked about the bad news. While most leaders will not want to do this, they will have to (at one time or another) play *politician*. This does not mean you have to put on two faces every time you walk out your office door (and I am not saying that all politicians have two faces, or am I?). What I am saying is sometimes you have to do what you have to do. At the same time, I am not advocating you have to lie to avoid dealing with the bad news – whether you know something or not.

I am advocating that you might have to deliver an answer that no one wants to hear. It may go something like this: "That's not what I am here for" or "You might need to talk to your supervisor one-on-one about that." However, it is extremely important that you never use your role as a *Walking Leader* as a vehicle to propagate those rumors. Under no circumstances should you fall into the trap of *"being one of the guys"* and start, spread, or

reshape a rumor. Instead, you have to do what you can to stop any rumor in its tracks. While *"being one of the guys"* may make you popular with the break room crowd, it will all but destroy your authenticity, trust and loyalty to your peers and those superiors who are already dealing with a bad situation.

Just remember: You will not always be able to bring good news when you are walking about. Therefore, when there is bad news it would be prudent to shift to observer mode. However, when you have good news, tell everyone, tell the world.

Rule #10
Catch Them In The Act Of Doing Something Right

People will always surprise you. When you least expect it, they will go and do something that will catch you completely without warning. Unfortunately, bad individuals or bad incidents sometimes force those employees who do something good into the shadows thus they are easily overlooked. In one case, it was a young, inexperienced, half-asleep Army private pulling guard duty who caught his commanding officer trying to sneak into a restricted area. The young private was in my squad and, as new privates usually do, got the crappiest guard shift, the middle of the night shift. All of us knew there might be a problem with him possibly falling asleep on duty, as he had done so on more than one occasion during the day. However, as it turns out, this young infantryman took his duty so seriously that he did not hesitate to "capture" someone who was trying to sneak into the ammo tent. During the attempt to capture the culprit, the two made such a ruckus that everyone thought the private had gotten himself into a fight with a "Grune-pig" (feral pig). After the dust settled, he had captured our commanding officer. The commanding officer was so impressed with the private, especially considering that no one had come to his aid during the scuffle, that he gave the soldier a three-day pass. The rest of us got an extra day out in the field for not going to the aid of the guard. Oh, the commander certainly caught everyone doing something – and nothing, all right.

When you are out walking, be sure to catch people in the act of doing something right, something good. Tell them you saw it and you appreciate what they did and it will not go unrecognized. Some organizations go out of their way to catch people doing something wrong, even if it is unintentionally wrong. I find it surprising that some organizations in the 21st century still give the impression that they hire individuals only to fire them. It makes no sense to me and it should make no sense to those organizations, yet they keep doing it. Sadly, those organizations thrive on chaos. The kind of chaos that comes from having absolutely no problem slaughtering their lambs while the wolves continue to roam the corporate countryside. Therefore, it is up to you to be the "anti-lamb slayer" and become one of the few who catches people doing something right and positive.

Whether it is taking extra time with a client or ensuring that the new employees are up to speed with the rest of the tenured staff, it's that exceptional something extra that you are looking for. Rest assured your organization has employees doing good things. They do good things all the time but it is the exceptional that you have to really look for. Just as they go out of their way to do the exceptional, you must go out of your way to catch the organization's staff doing just that.

Of course, you will also come across someone doing something wrong. As a leader, you are expected to report the incident or if necessary address the situation immediately. This does not make you a snitch or a fraud; this makes you authentic. Failing to report any wrongdoing will certainly make you two things: someone who cannot be counted on and a genuine liability to your organization.

As to not become a liability, you must do what you can to not be in a situation of catching someone doing something wrong and not doing something about it. Do not turn a blind eye to anything that is not in line with the organization's way of doing things. You must be just as

adamant when it comes to finding something good as when you come across something bad happening. If you decide that looking away is the best thing for you to do while attempting to be a Walking Leader then please do not bother starting or continuing any further. Close this book, right now. Drop me an email at dave@daveguerra.com, convince me why the best thing for you to do is to ignore the bad that is happening in your organization and I will gladly refund you the cost of this book.

Something to remember – and it is definitely in your favor and in the favor of the organization – is that consistent walking around will minimize the chances of catching people doing something wrong and increase the chances of catching them doing something right. Simply put, being highly visible and available will further the need for staff to do things the right way, and doing things the wrong way will become more difficult.

When you catch people doing something right, what do you do? You tell everyone, especially their supervisor and their supervisor's supervisor. You can do

this through an email or, better yet, send a quick handwritten note. You do remember writing, right?

Writing a note goes a long way; it not only represents recognition of something good, but it also shows that you are genuine in what you are doing, what your message is, and what you think of the people that you are working with. Lastly and most importantly, it tells the individual that you honored and immortalized their action by handwriting them a little something. Yes, a handwritten note is that important, especially in this age of texts and tweets.

As the simple act of catching people in the act of doing something good will go a long way, I offer this tip: Do not go looking for something good the first few times out on your walking journey. Wait a while; get a feel for what is good and what is expected, then go out and find the exceptionally good stuff.

Rule #11
Correct On The Spot

Correcting on the spot was, for the longest time, one of those things that I saw as a "should I" or "shouldn't I" and not "I must." That lasted until I was in a situation to prevent something terrible from happening. Early in my current career, I was at one of our contract field sites and noticed the staff were all but ignoring someone who obviously needed our assistance. I asked the field site lead why the individual in the waiting room was not being helped. The site lead told me she did not understand "whatever" language the individual was speaking. My response, "so are you going to ignore her and hope she goes away?" The site lead noticed the disappointment in the tone of my voice. She said they were waiting for someone to help translate. "Does the lady know this?" I asked. The lead said they were able to communicate that through hand gestures.

"Are you sure she understood you?"

"I think so."

This was the last straw. I told the site lead I did not want to hear "I think so" anymore. I wanted to hear "I know" or "I don't know," but "I think so" is out.

So how do we find out if the woman understood the hand gestures? I enlightened the site lead that Google Translator is a good tool, when nothing or no one else can help, to help find out and know. I called the woman over to the counter and using Google Translator was able to have a rough but understood Tagalog-English conversation. I have instructed all my staff to use translation tools when absolutely necessary and only for superficial communication, not for getting into details of doing business, because something may get lost in translation and that would not be a good thing.

While you are out, you will at times encounter situations or individuals operating outside the expectations of the organization. There are only two sides that are outside the organization's performance expectations: very good and very bad. In the previous chapter, we talked about what to do when you catch employees doing something very good. However, now you have to look at what to do when you catch someone doing something very bad.

Short of the employee(s) being in the middle of an emergency, at which time it is all hands on deck, you stop everything that is happening, locate the offender(s) and correct on the spot. Make certain that while correcting on the spot you do so in a manner that is not critical. Of course, you are calling someone out because of something they did or failed to do, remember that while you might not come across as being critical; to that individual employee it will most certainly feel like the world coming down on them. Ensure that you are only there to help and that they know you are only there to help in preventing a bad situation from getting worse.

As previously mentioned, there will be a time that you will come across someone doing something wrong, even when you are looking for someone doing something right. Depending on how wrong it is, the action you take will most certainly depend on the policies and procedures of your organization. Usually the far more grievous situations, such as sexual harassment or fraud are addressed at a higher level and with more urgency. While minor infractions are usually based on misunderstandings or misinterpretations of policies and procedures and while must be dealt with the level of urgency may vary greatly.

It will be necessary to document and report everything that happens, ensure that you do so every time. While all infractions carry some form of consequence and typically minor ones don't carry a punishment of suspension or termination, if your organization has a disciplinary action specifically for certain types of minor infractions, then you are bound, as a manager and leader, to address them in the manner prescribed by the organization's policy and procedures.

What does this mean? It means you have permission to take care of business, especially if there is something wrong with the way business is done. In every agency, company or organization there is an expectation that everyone will do the right thing, so do not think that you cannot take care of things as you are walking around, especially when walking around in other departments. Remember, you are not walking around to find things that are wrong, but when you do find them, you are expected to address them in a professional manner.

As I wrote about correcting on the spot: DON'T BE CRITICAL.

While it might sound easy, this will be difficult to achieve and even more difficult to master. Nevertheless, it can be done. In fact, it must be done and mastered by anyone who takes himself seriously as a leader. Unfortunately, leaders sometimes make unpopular decisions. Thus, when it comes time to correct on the spot, knowing how to effectively address what needs to be corrected is critical, especially when it is going to be the most unpopular thing you have ever done. Knowing how to correct on the spot will help minimize any long-term effects of doing something "unpopular."

Before you go correcting on the spot, I recommend that you take a moment and study how to observe, orient, decide, and act (OODA), otherwise known as the OODA Loop. The OODA Loop is one of many tools that can be used when it comes to correcting on the spot while not to being overly critical, because it forces you to pause and fully assess the situation before initiating any form of correction.

The OODA Loop is the brainchild of U.S. Air Force Colonel John Boyd (1927–1997), and is used not only in the military but also in the business world. The OODA

Loop takes the four components, each acting upon the other, to make good things happen. Dissecting the OODA Loop:

- OBSERVE: This component calls on the individual to collect as much information as possible regarding what the employee is doing and why it is wrong.

- ORIENT: Orienting yourself to who, what, where, when, why and how of the situation can be a little tricky, as it involves determining the capabilities of the employee, such as tenure, position, training, and known skill set. In most cases, it also involves ascertaining the tenure, position, training and known skill set of those present.

- DECIDE: Reach a conclusion, or plan of action, if you will, regarding what you will do to remedy the situation. As you gathered the necessary information, processed and oriented yourself to the situation, you can now formulate a suitable plan of action. As correcting on the spot in most cases takes place after the situation has unfolded, you have the luxury of taking time to collect the necessary data and developing a plan of action. However, there will be times when you will deal with a situation as it is unfolding, therefore you will have to act quickly. Do not give up too much when acting quickly; stay focused and do not become rattled by the speed at which things are happening.

- ACT: Now is the time to put your decision into action. Make the correction by first ensuring that the employee(s) and you recognize what was done wrong, how it should be done correctly, and then ensure that the staff member(s) can do it correctly on their own. If problems persist, meet immediately with the employee's immediate supervisor and your organization's trainer, if you have one, and have a "corrective" plan of action in place before moving the problem up the chain of command. Remember: It is ALWAYS better to bring a solution to the problem you are reporting to a supervisor or superior.

As always, check your organization's policies and procedures so as not to get yourself in trouble when correcting on the spot. However, you have my permission to go out there and correct on the spot when it is absolutely warranted and not for the sake of having the authority to correct others. You have permission to do the right thing when it comes to helping others do the right thing.

Rule #12
Make Sure It's Not All Business

There is a time and place for everything. However, all work and no play does make Johnny a dull boy. Why not mix a little levity into an already stressful day? There is plenty of stress in most modern workplaces, but I feel like I am preaching to the choir. Earlier I mentioned the shutdown-that-never-was as Hurricane Alex approached. Yet, there was plenty of downtime when the rains kept customer-facing activities to a minimum. There were power outages; none lasted very long but there was downtime nonetheless. During these times, I had to do something to break the tension of the frustration of not being able to work because the power was out. This was the perfect time to get to know each other a little better, so I asked, "What do you normally do when the power goes out at home?" The first response came from an accounting clerk: "Well, if it's during the day we start thinking about cooking dinner on the barbecue pit." The conversation took off from there. We discussed work, spouses, kids, bills and work. Power was restored within the hour, but during that downtime we fostered deeper relationships with each other. While being forced not to work certainly gave us an opportunity that normally would not be afforded to us. However, since that time and up until I left my job with the State of Texas, every chance we had we made certain that it was not all about work.

One the most dangerous things to do is to make your walks all about business. If you do not show some of your soft side or human side and are rigid every time you leave your office, it's difficult for others to open up to you. Walking around stiff and always meaning business will put people on guard, which leads to them putting up a wall that you will have to work just that much harder to tear down. It does not have to be this way.

Doing all that you can to ensure your walks are not all about business is one of the easiest rules any Walking Leader can follow. This, on the contrary, does not mean that you are walking out on the frontlines to kill time, especially the employees' time; you will have to be careful to not abuse this rule.

How does one ensure that as a Walking Leader you are not all business? For starters, make your Monday morning walk one that helps diffuse the stress that

Monday always bring. Keep the conversation light so the distraction you create will not be that bad, too big or too deep. This helps keep the employees somewhat on task without being overly distracted. Some will argue that any distraction is too much. I disagree, and there is no greater distraction than Monday with its "Why is the weekend so short?" "Did you catch the game?" and the ever popular "How was your weekend?" Each question can lead to long drawn-out discussions regarding who had the better weekend and so on.

Throughout the business day, staff will need to get up and stretch a bit so they do not get bored to the point of distraction, so an occasional diversion is not only allowed but also expected. Thus, it is OK to not be just all about business. Get out there, break the ice and start a conversation.

If you are not too sure how to start a light conversation, here are few icebreakers to get the ball rolling:

- *How are the kids? (If you know they have them)*

- *Did you see any of the football games this past weekend? (Or any other sport in season)*

- *How about them Astros? (May vary on the sports season or the local favorite pro sports team)*

- *Did you see that new movie? (Insert the name of the latest release that you saw)*

Something important to remember: do not interrupt when the employee is answering your questions. Then again, it is just as important to not interrupt when the employee is with a client. Wait until later or come back tomorrow, but under no circumstances should you interrupt while the staff member is performing her duties, especially those duties and assignments that require plenty of attention to detail and cannot be put off.

Getting to know people is the best way to gain the trust of those you do not supervise. The line between you being there only for work and you being there for everyone will not be as thick as it was initially perceived – and that's a good thing. Of course, you will have to do some homework. You will have to watch and keep up with the latest sporting events, watch the latest motion picture, and visit some of the newest attractions in your area. While you might find it fun to do, remember it is all about having something to talk about come Monday morning – and the rest of the week.

Rule #13
You Are Not A Spy

Those working in the IT industry are sometimes considered "hackers" by those who have a little trouble fully grasping what a network analyst or network support technician does and does not do. They especially have difficulty understanding whom they are working for. Unfortunately, there will be those times when people will just flat out accuse an IT person of reading their emails without their permission or "hacking" into their work PCs for some dubious reason or another. As the lead IT person for my region, I was not immune to such accusations, especially when individuals were caught with their hands in the cookie jar and were looking for a way to save themselves. Sometimes it was just to deflect attention from the real problem; themselves. Having the keys to the digital castle made my staff and me easy targets. Of course, I was shocked the first time such accusations arose but this served as a catalyst to do something to change their perception of my department, my staff and me. I got out there and started to get to know my co-workers. As soon as they realized I was actually there to help, people started to feel more at ease and less suspect.

You are not there to be a spy. You should never give the impression that you are spying to your peers, your supervisors and, most of all, to the employees you encounter during your walks. For any program to work, especially one that involves managers interacting with employees other than their own, this concept or rule is important in creating authenticity. This is also a rule that will be the most difficult for all employees at all levels to understand and accept. It is also a rule that will come into its own over time.

As I mentioned, staff will be suspicious of your actions and activities right from the start. This is normal and expected. Rest assured, over time this attitude will change, provided you are not doing this to spy on your peers and those who work around and under you. If you are using the *Walking Leader* as a tool to become a spy then I ask you to please STOP right now and proceed no further. This is not what being a leader is about.

How does a leader convince others that her intentions are purely what she says they are? Simple:

always be authentic and transparent in how you interact with others. Be genuine and with purposeful intent in your actions. However, there will be times when you will have to show them that you will have to do things that may appear "spy"-like especially when reporting something that has gone wrong. As mentioned in Rule #11 (*Correct on the Spot*) you will encounter incidents and situations where you will have to step into corrective action mode and address what must be addressed. This does not mean that you were out there with the intention of finding something wrong; this just means you stepped in when the situation called for you to step in. Such situations could range from simple safety infractions to filling out the wrong form for a client.

A word of caution: To third-party observers it may appear that what you are doing is spying. Usually, these observers are individuals who are not familiar with what you are doing, or they are customers who have limited interaction with you, your organization or with any of its employees. Do not sweat it; there will come a time when those employees will know exactly what is happening and they will be able to truly understand what you are doing and why.

As I have tried to emphasize, to overcome the sense of being considered a spy, you must have patience and understanding. Know that being consistent will help minimize the impression of spying. However, there will be people (employees, peers, and even superiors) who will consider you a spy and not be quiet about what they think. There is no need to confront anyone in an effort to convert them. Confronting anyone is not a path you want to take especially with anyone who does not believe your intentions are honorable. All that confrontation will do is to make them even more suspicious of you. If you really want to do something to attempt to convert someone, all you have to do is act! Your actions will be all the proof that anyone – and everyone – will need to know you are not the spy others are making you out to be.

Rule #14
Employees Must Know You Are Available

When I started my post-State job, I was in learning mode. I knew the business and what it entailed but I did not fully understand the day-to-day operation stuff. I still had to master the "meat and potatoes" of the business and of doing business before I would even consider myself at some level of operating competence. I would visit all the contract sites to get a feel for how things were done the same and what things were done differently. I would sometimes not say anything but observe how the staff were doing their thing, then leave. At first, the employees would want to initiate a conversation with the new guy and I would answer but I had to keep it brief because I was there to observe and learn. I gave myself a hard deadline of 90 days to get fully up to speed and jump in. Of course, 90 days can be a lifetime in the business world and some organizations cannot wait that long. I was fortunate that the company had been doing business for 15 years, so the processes could continue and could wait for me to be truly well-versed. On the 91st day, I met with all the employees and told them that my probation was over. I was now in it up to my chin and I was in it with them. At that meeting, I also told them I would now be available to them 100%. They were now able to contact me by phone; I was to be their primary point of contact when they called in sick, needed supplies delivered or anything. Being distant and reserved during my acclimation period of those first 90 days, I had to be that obvious and blatant in telling them.

Every employee must know you are available when you are out and about. This is a non-negotiable rule as well as being one of the most difficult to master. Unfortunately, it is also extremely easily abused by you and the employees you encounter. Early on, you must draw a line when it comes to employees knowing you are available and employees using that availability for purposes other than work-related activities. This is when the abuse may occur. Therefore, it is imperative that you set some boundaries right from the beginning.

If they have other managers or supervisors, they need to understand that your availability is not a tool that can be used to circumvent their manager or supervisor, nor is it a tool that will be used to get you to interdict on their behalf in situations involving performance or personnel issues. That is strictly reserved for the employee's chain of command, of which they might have to be reminded. If you are in the chain of command then you are already in the loop. If you are not in the employee's direct chain of command, then you must ensure that what you are told stays confidential. As you can see, this is the one path that when followed can quickly be abused and you do not want to go there.

However, being available and fully ensuring that the employees know you will be available is something that can only be achieved over time. When they get used to you being present and available they will start to understand how available you truly are. Of course, your walking around time should not be the only time you are available.

You will have to be available all the time. However, you can emphasize the priority of your availability is dedicated to the Walking Leader time spent on the floor, in the trenches, out on the frontlines, etc. Of course, those who want more time from you, or dedicated time, can always call your extension or drop you an email.

Reassure them that they can always get hold of you whether you are in or out of the office.

A word (or two) of warning: Never let people know you are uninterested in them or show any sense of boredom in what they say. Word will spread faster than a California wildfire that what was once genuine is now a *fraud* and no longer worth anyone's time. The employees will feel betrayed and WILL LOSE FAITH IN YOU and what you are doing. No matter how boring or how uninterested you really are keep it buried deep inside of you, never, ever let them see you show that disinterest.

Side note: While you are encouraged to leave your electronic tethers in your office, especially when you start your Walking Leader adventures, this should not prevent employees from contacting you. Most organizations (well, most cool organizations) now have email addresses for all employees. If they want you to stop by, they can email you ahead of your departure from your office. If some individuals have a difficult time contacting you or remembering your email address, why not carry some "special" business cards made exclusively for in-house use with you?

TIP: If your organization provides just one type of business card and you would like to have some special, business cards made that will not break the bank, go to the Moo.com website (www.moo.com) and check out their line of fully customizable mini-cards. They might just be exactly what you need.

Rule #15
Solicit And Act On Suggestions

When you work for the State of Texas, the U.S. Army or any large organization, change is not something that can happen overnight. Usually, things are a little different in the private sector. Depending on the size of the organization, change can happen in as little as a couple of hours. The levels of middle managers, committees, focus groups and other bureaucratic nonsense may make change feel like a tire that has a very slow leak. You know the tire is leaking but you do nothing until you have a tire that is flat on the bottom. I feel good knowing that now I actively solicit feedback and suggestions from all of the organization's staff members. There are times when we can act immediately, such as when it comes to ensuring that procedures and protocols are in place to further protect the customer's privacy and rights. While working for the state agency there was some latitude afforded the local and regional managers, but that latitude was very limited in scope and implementation had to remain extremely localized. Unfortunately, when something happened that required massive change, the process was long and drawn out. If the reputation of the agency was run through the mud along the way, so be it. It was frustrating knowing that change – for the better – was taking so very long to happen, let alone having to be approved to begin to happen. However, that did not stop me from continuing to ask questions or solicit comments, ideas, and suggestions from everyone I encountered during my walks. Most people would ask for the moon knowing full well that they would not get what they wanted. I will say this: Each and every one of those state employees was glad to have someone care enough to ask for their input and know that someone would move it up the chain of command. It has been a bumpy road, but it is so good to be in a position to make things happen. And making things happen quickly is priceless.

Soliciting and acting on suggestions involves complete interaction between all parties concerned. To effectively solicit and act on those suggestions, go to the source. In this case, the source is those who are on the frontlines: the employees. This should be no problem because you are out there as part of your walks already.

While it may have been some time since you were active on the frontlines, rest assured things HAVE changed. Why? Because someone is always thinking of a new way to build a better mousetrap and builds it. Someone is always thinking that if they were in charge they would do something differently and they do. Now, here is your opportunity to help those employees who feel they cannot build a better mousetrap, even though they know they can. When you ask for suggestions you become their voice to the top because, depending on the tenure of some of the staff, they might feel their opportunity to make change happen has come and gone. By being there and actively interested in them, you become their second chance at an opportunity. You now stand to make new ROCK STARS within your organization. You are set to become a STAR maker by soliciting suggestions from those employees who would otherwise not have the chance to express them.

Another word of caution: Be careful what you ask for, because you might just get it and then some. Therefore, you should at least know which suggestions are valid and which just cannot be implemented. This does not mean that you shoot down the crazy ideas. Remember, the Rubik's Cube, the Pet Rock and Chia Pets were once crazy ideas. Look at the phenomena they turned out to be. So, do not be hasty to shoot down any idea that is really out of the box. Who knows? You might be staring the next Rubik's Cube right in the eye!

Seriously, nothing is better than being the one who discovers the organization's next "Rock Star". This then leads us to the next point: Giving credit where credit is due. While you might be the one who takes those great ideas to the organization's leadership, you have to ensure those individuals who came up with the suggestions are given the proper credit and compensated. This ensures that a conduit for future suggestions and ideas works and stays open.

Rule #16
Promote Others To Do The Same

The benefits of teamwork were instilled in me right from the start of my military career. We were taught that we could either sink or swim, we could succeed or fail, and no matter what happened during basic training we would be in it together. We were a team, a team of 36 young men. All of us made my training platoon in 1985 out among the red clay of Fort Benning, Georgia. Luckily, my cohorts and I made it past Basic and Advanced Infantry Training, and just as quickly as we formed into a cohesive and dangerous group of Infantrymen, we were split up and shipped off to the far corners of the planet or wherever Uncle Sam needed us. My subsequent assignments, jobs, duties and commitments would all have a solid foundation based on teamwork, as it was the ONLY way of successfully achieving what we did together. In encouraging others to get out there and get to know their co-workers, I tell them that's the only way that the front-line staff will know you have their back. Having someone's back means, they trust you enough to let you have their back and that's a good thing. Remember when you were on the frontlines, you needed someone to look up to, to mentor and guide you. Some people were lucky enough to have that person, while sadly others did not. Heck, I can't even begin to remember just how many foxholes I dug, but I do know that I started out on the frontlines and that's where my roots are and always will be. I also know there were some great non-commissioned officers (NCOs) and commissioned officers who lent a hand or two along the way. Whom in turn, inspired me to return the favor to those I now lead, supervise and encounter. I hope I am inspiring others to do the same, in the future when they are in a position to do so. There will always be skeptics when it comes to promoting others to do the same as I do. They usually have their own agenda or have felt wronged by the system, the process, other managers, or whatever the reason. It is unfortunate, because they also make the loudest noise, and they could easily turn that negativity outward and work for the common good instead of issuing threats of going to the press or calling a state legislator the moment something does not go right for the individual, and never giving the team a second thought. Every organization – public or private – has at least one individual like that. Mine did. His negativity brought the whole place down but I did not let that deter me. I continued pressing others to ignore him and do what was right. To me, ignoring his idle threats was the best course of action, because sometimes, as I like to quote from Star Trek II: Wrath of Khan: "Logic clearly dictates that the needs of the many outweigh the needs of the few" or the one.

Promote others to do the same. Initially, this will be rather difficult to do, especially if your peers have never given any thought to the idea of walking around and being among the front-line staff on a regular basis. Most certainly, B-schools are teaching tactics such as getting out there among the "troops" and spouting the virtues of doing so. These tactics can be directly applied almost immediately after starting with a new organization. However, there are many trains of thought on how to effectively make and sustain authentic relationships. The Walking Leader is the one who encompasses all that is out there and more. So, as long as you continue to persevere in believing that being a Walking Leader is the right thing to do, it will be. Recruiting others will be that much easier.

Remember, it is just plain human nature for one to be skeptical of anything new or untried or untested. If you are one of the first within your organization to be a Walking Leader, then you as the pioneer will have an even more difficult task when it comes to recruiting others. It is essential to stay the course with making walking around your organization a habit. I defer to the late Dr. Stephen Covey and his bestselling book *The 8th Habit* where he states: "It takes 21 days to form a habit." So don't give up! Don't ever give up!

Eventually, your peers, subordinates, superiors and others will get used to seeing you walking around, they will ask questions, and they will become curious as to what you are doing and how they can do it too. This, of course, will promote the Walking Leader as something that everyone can do, not just managers or those in leadership positions. Those who are up-and-coming within the organization will take to the Walking Leader with minimal prodding, while others will need that little extra push to get them on board. This is a good thing, because the more who hop on the bandwagon, the more your organization's communication and professionalism levels will increase. Having an organization that is professional, open and can communicate at all levels and across all levels will certainly deliver a sizeable return on the Walking Leader investment (time and relationships) and eventually positively impact the company's bottom line.

When you are promoting others to do the same, please ensure they know and understand that it will be a difficult process, especially at first. Though you may have been the pathfinder, their journey towards becoming a master Walking Leader will be long and difficult. You will have to show all three sides of the Walking Leader: the good as well as the bad and most certainly the ugly. This will benefit those who decide to set out on their own Walking Leader adventure, because you will have NOT painted a rosy picture but a very realistic image. For all the good and bad that is to come, you will become their "accidental mentor" because you will be the person they go to when they encounter problems or setbacks during the entire process.

Rule #17
Be Visible

The thing I disliked the most during my military career were the few individuals (enlisted, non-commissioned officers and commissioned officers) who went out of their way to catch someone doing something wrong – sneaking around in the dark or hiding just around the corner to overhear conversations, baiting younger soldiers to get themselves in trouble, and so on. Now, don't get me wrong. I'm not saying all of them were like that. I would say there were maybe one or two in every unit who behaved this way. Some were obvious, while others were so sneaky that the only way a young soldier found out was when it was too late. That behavior served no purpose other than to create animosity against and distrust of the leadership because it was passively or actively condoned. I knew this was something I would never do if I were ever in any kind of position of leadership and trust. When I achieved that level of trust within the State of Texas agency I worked for, and in the private sector, I knew there was only one way to go. It was the most difficult thing to accomplish but I made certain that when I was out there

I was visible and there was no doubt about what I was doing.
Now if others saw it differently, well that was on them.

Being visible is another rule that is easy and difficult at the same time. At first, you will be tempted to fly under the leadership's radar. However, this is not good, flying under the radar will create suspicion that something underhanded or covert may be going on. It would behoove you to not fly under any radar at any time. For this same reason, I am not advocating that you shout your intentions from the rooftops. Just get out there and do it. Step outside your office door and just start walking. As that famous slogan from that famous shoe company goes: *"Just Do It."*

To help with this visibility, I recommend putting in your calendar that you will be active at specific times and dates. If you use iCal, Microsoft Outlook, Google Calendar or any other shared calendar or scheduling application, be certain that you put your time on the floor there for all to see. You do not have to go into detail as to the aspects of what you are doing, because initially you are still trying to figure out what you will be doing. For that matter, you might still not fully know what you are doing after months, if not years, of walking around the organization. That's a good thing; it may show that the organization is continually changing and change is good for everyone.

When the time comes, and it will sooner than you think, you will be asked to explain what you are doing and why. Simply, say you are walking around, which is the truth and nothing but the truth. Of course, at that time, reveal as much as you are comfortable revealing. It is understandable; initially you might not come across as 100% certain of what you are doing. That is OK. As has been an underlying theme throughout this book: BE PATIENT. Over time, you will see the confidence in what you are doing increase and you will effectively answer any and all questions regarding the Walking Leader and what you are doing with it, as well as how you are personalizing or customizing it to suit the way things are done within the organization.

At the beginning, you may be tempted to lay low and hide at the beginning. Fight the temptation fight it at all cost. Stand tall and take it one-step at a time. You are embarking on a journey that will last the rest of your career within your organization, as well as when you move up the organization's career ladder or move to a different company. At that point, you will be in a position to guide and mentor others on how you were able to get to where you are.

Rule #18
Be Genuine. Be Authentic.

Over the years, I have seen many wonderful people be themselves. They are being genuine and they are authentic. I have seen them remain true to their word, and committed to what they believe in. They do not pull any punches. Then again, I have also seen some of the most horrifying thoughts, words and deeds that people could possess or do. They scared me; they made me wonder how they could reach those depths. In some cases, I could not wrap my head around how they got that way. How they can have such deep-rooted paranoia, mania, and a most disturbing mindset, yet could hide it so well. Sometimes it is difficult to see people for who they really are. Then again, sometimes all you have to do is scratch the surface. Remember, I am not a practicing psychologist nor do I play one on TV so I will not begin to go into the psychoanalytical reasons for what drives such people. I do know one thing: I have seen many people afraid to admit they need help, so much so that they have lost their career, their family, and the trust of the people who love them the most. While assigned the US Army in Berlin, I had the pleasure of meeting a young officer, a second lieutenant, who arrived full of fire and gusto but also had a love for the party life. I guess it was difficult for him to let go of the college "frat" life. This guy worked hard, played hard and partied even harder. This was his way for a while. That is, until one day he was gone. In the military, if you are quickly removed from a unit you obviously did something very, very wrong. I found out later that his drinking and partying caught up with him. The sad part of this story is that all he had to do was admit he had a problem, wanted help, and this young officer's career would still be intact. I believe he would have been one of the great officers; he had that charisma that the soldiers really liked, but now we will never really know. Since the start of my adult life, there have been many people who have served as examples of what not to do. Luckily, there have been even more people who have shown me what I should be doing right. Yet, in my mind, the cautionary tales always seem to stick out the most. Don't they always stick out the most? Those cautionary tales are the ones that serve as the catalyst for me to continue to work hard to be a good example for my children, my family, my peers, and my co-workers.

Be Genuine and Be Authentic. Much like all the other rules, this rule will be one of the most difficult as well as the easiest. It will be easy for most first-time managers because they are full of energy and have the willingness to change the world. This might not be the case for seasoned managers who have encountered a few difficulties over the years. The veterans of the organization have seen leadership programs come and go, and they are more suspect of anything that goes against what they have been taught or learned the hard way. The concepts behind the Walking Leader are hardly new, but in a world loaded with 7 Habits, TQM, ISO 9000, Six Sigma, and so on and so on, the Walking Leader is not formally on the map, but the core concepts are.

This should not deter anyone from doing it. If anything, the Walking Leader should be used in conjunction with any process improvement systems your organization is currently using. Ultimately, it will come down to the individual, you, who is walking around. It comes down to where the steel meets the target (a.k.a. the frontlines of the organization).

In all of this, the key factor is and always will be to be yourself. In being yourself, you will have no choice but to be genuine and authentic. For some, it will be easier than for others. Some people have a natural ability to be themselves no matter the situation. This is not to say that no one else can be natural. Everyone is natural, but when you are in front of people the ability to be natural can become frankly unnatural (think "stage fright"). As with everything else mentioned, do not let this "unnatural" capability stop you from getting out in front of people. Please know this is not an open invitation to be "all in someone's face." Instead, it is an invitation to relax and be yourself. Keep it up, stay true to what you want to accomplish and eventually you will stop trying to *force* yourself to be yourself and you will just naturally be yourself.

For those who do not possess that natural ability to come across as genuine – and you know who you are – maybe you are just trying too hard. This is not going to turn into a section about the psychology of how one should carry one's self, but you may need to ask yourself some difficult questions and see what you are doing that is causing you to not come across as genuine and authentic to others.

Usually, if you can answer the following question, you'll know what you are doing wrong: How can I tell if someone is not genuine and authentic? After you answer that question, then ask yourself (and be truthful) if you are guilty of committing that which you just answered. If you answered YES, you have your work cut out for you.

Whether you are a long-term member of the organization or a first-timer, a great responsibility has been given to you and it is up to you to use it wisely. Remain genuine and authentic at all times and you will start to get back nothing less than genuine and authentic from those you encounter in your walks. Ultimately, that is what you and the organization want, especially in this age of openness and transparency. Achieving full openness and transparency is a symbol of success and that is what the Walking Leader is about.

Rule #19
Be Patient

Humans do not like to be patient, and managers are no exception. In any organization, public or private, things happen quickly and being patient definitely goes against the grain of what you have been taught and are expected to do. If you are a manager who is starting on the Walking Leader program of getting out there, you must rewire, reconfigure or reconstruct yourself, your way of thinking, and your expectations. This ensures you do not expect too much too soon. Results will happen over time with small successes at the beginning. Once small successes occur the larger ones follow, something like a snowball rolling down a hill accumulating more snow along the way.

Throughout this book, patience and being patient is the running theme. It is so very important that you fully understand that you cannot rush something that refuses to be – or cannot be – rushed. As you undertake this process, understand and know that the Walking Leader is not only about "going the distance" or about "being in it to win it," but is about pacing yourself. Always remember that the Walking Leader never was and never will be a 100-yard dash. It can be best described as more like a marathon that forces you to pace yourself if you want to finish it.

Running 26.2 miles at a full sprint will do nothing but burn you out faster than a candle in hurricane winds. Running a marathon is about holding a steady pace all the way to the end. Keeping that steady pace will not only get you to the finish line but it will get you there with your sanity and body all in one piece. It would be safe to say that many of us have heard the old saying: *"Rome wasn't built in a day"* and while it may be a tired saying, it is very true. The same goes with becoming a successful leader within the organization.

A fantastic example of taking time to build successful leaders is the United States Army. The U.S. Army and the other military branches have created the epitome of leadership that corporate America has attempted to emulate for a long time. They have come close but cannot exactly duplicate the U.S. Army's leadership development program. The precursor to the modern U.S. Army was the Continental Army. Back in 1775, the Continental Army consisted of an all-volunteer force, much like today's military. Then the force consisted of civilians that put aside their professions such as blacksmiths, farmers, deckhands, lawyers and just about any occupation that existed throughout the original 13 colonies to fight for our nation's independence from England.

At the time the Continental Army was established, there were very few professional soldiers in its ranks. The professionals were either for the most part men who had completed their obligation to His Majesty's Royal Army, or traitors who would rather fight with the colonials and risk execution, if captured by the British. Early in the Revolutionary War, the Continental Army garnered some great victories, but the successes came at a high price for an Army that was mostly composed of men who were professionals by their choice of vocation and not professional soldiers.

Today, the United States Armed Forces has the luxury of something called Basic Training (Boot Camp), which some 200-plus years ago did not exist, at least in the formal sense. In order to win the war against the British, General George Washington had no choice but to turn his ragtag group of citizen "soldiers" into a force that would to defeat the British and lead to the birth of a new nation without fail. Up to this point, the new nation was a country on paper and had very little to show beyond that. General Washington tasked ex-Prussian officer Baron Friedrich Wilhelm Ludolf Gerhard Augustin von Steuben, yes that Baron Von Steuben, to turn the citizens into soldiers.

Baron von Steuben took about 100 select colonials and trained them. He trained them until they became the cadre (managers) who went on to train the rest of the Continental Army. To this day, the U.S. Army continues basic training somewhat the same way Baron von Steuben did with those early American heroes. Therefore, by having vision and patience, General Washington took those citizens of the colonies who chose to fight to create a nation, and turned them into soldiers. You know how that story ended.

However, it was not that cut and dry. General Washington endured setbacks that seemed to give everyone the impression that all would soon be lost. One of the problems was that, unlike the modern military where most of the recruits are in their late teens to early twenties, the patriots of the Continental Army were older and set in their ways of doing things. This made von Steuben's task long and arduous, but in the end the nation's right to exist was assured after the Continental Army's victory with the surrender of the British at Yorktown.

There will be times when you will get discouraged, as things do not seem to be progressing. Do not give up! There will certainly be days when you do not see anything good happening but there will be days that are going to be full of the good stuff. Tempted as you may be, do not give up! As you go along, the good days will definitely begin to outnumber the bad. Being consistent and vigilant when conducting your walks around the organization will all but ensure that every action you take, now, is one that shows your professionalism, your management skills and, above all, your ability to lead and be a leader people will follow without reservation. Never give up!

Rule #20
Have Fun!

Have fun!

Nothing more needs to be said about this rule.

However, if something does need to be said then know this: If you are not having fun then you are most certainly doing it wrong or you are not doing it consistently. Worse still, you are not doing it at all.

The solution is quite simple: It is time to start all over.

Then see Rule #1.

However, if you are having fun, then you are doing it right.

But you can do better, you can always do better. See Rule #1.

Of course, you can choose to stop at any time and restart anytime you want. There is NO perfect duration to master any one of these rules. Heck, you might never master any of them or you might master all of them. Whether you do or do not, there is no set time limit to get from Rule #1 to Rule #20 and there is certainly no rule that says you have to follow the rules of the Walking Leader in the order you read them.

I hope that you have first read this book and then implement Col. John Boyd's OODA Loop to get yourself ready to take the first step out of your office and onto your organization's frontlines. Once you decide to start, please use this handy-dandy book as a guide that you can refer back to when things start to slip, but don't get lazy. Being lazy will make it difficult to get yourself back on track. You will not only have to run the OODA Loop on issues and conflicts, but you will have to use it as a tool to keep yourself in check.

Now get out there and be the Leader you know you can be!

Best Wishes and Good Luck!

Resources

BIBLIOGRAPHY

Covey, Stephen. *The 8th Habit Personal Workbook*. New York: Free Press, 2006. 117. Print.

OODA Loop. (2013, May 31). In Wikipedia, The Free Encyclopedia. Retrieved 03:48, June 4, 2013, from http://en.wikipedia.org/w/index.php?title=OODA_loop&oldid=557624462

TOOLS & SUPPLIES YOU WILL NEED

CHAPTER 3: FIELD NOTES highly portable notebook can be found @ http://fieldnotesbrand.com/

CHAPTER 14: MOO MiniCards small double-sided cards you design @ http://us.moo.com/products/minicards.html

INK PENs: Always have and carry a very good ink pen. Pick one that suits your mission, your personality, and you. The prices can vary but is not a very good ink pen worth it? I recommend you visit Paradise Pen and browse their varied collection of pens. I am have a feeling they will have the right pen for you @

http://www.paradisepen.com/

Acknowledgments

Words can express only so much about how I feel about the people who helped me throughout this journey. This book's roots can be traced back to when I joined the US Army (July 1985) and there are many individuals and organizations I must thank. Like an Academy Award winner, I will keep this as brief as possible.

The biggest thanks go to my wife, Teresa, my children Emma and Matthew, and my Mother and Brothers. You will never know how much your support has meant to me.

Thanks to every soldier who ever served with the U.S. Army's Berlin Brigade (1945-1994). It is an honor to have served and be associated with such great soldiers and leaders.

Thank you to Donna Papacosta of Trafalgar Communications, who helped shape this book. Whether Donna wants to admit it or not, it was a comment she made during one of her podcast episodes that gave me the final push to finish this manuscript.

Last and not least: For those who have been with me over the years and whose names I have failed to mention, I ask your forgiveness, because you have truly helped me.

Thank You,

David Guerra

Biography

He was born in Texas, but Army brat David Guerra was not destined to roam the Lone Star State all his life. His father led him and his family to various military posts, and it was during his childhood and teenage years that David's thirst for adventure and travel began.

No one was surprised when David joined the U.S. Army as an Infantryman. His first duty assignment put him at the tip of the Cold War spear, 110 miles inside communist East German territory, in West Berlin.

In Berlin David's view of the world changed – especially that of the U.S. military inside the Berlin Wall during the Cold War. No longer was he just along for the ride with his father's assignments. Instead David was learning from great leaders and managers the skills, knowledge and wisdom that would be the foundation for his adult life long after leaving Berlin and the Army.

David went on to work for the State of Texas as a network analyst and eventually became an IT department manager. While working for the state, David completed his bachelor's and master's degrees in business administration, having decided it was best to work at gaining experience before going to school. Those years of experience combined with his education made David ready to deploy in the private sector. Now, he is in a position to influence not only his staff, but also everyone he encounters, on the path to becoming better individuals and leaders.

David and his wife, Teresa, are proud of their children, Emma and Matthew, and they love to travel back to Berlin whenever possible.